Your *Fabulous* is Showing

by
Sasha Gray

Glitter Dome Press

Published 2019 by Glitter Dome Press

All rights reserved. No part of this publication may be reproduced or transmitted in any form or by any means, including informational storage and retrieval systems, without permission in writing from the publisher, or author, except for brief quotations in a review. For permission requests, please contact Sasha Gray.

Printed 2019
Printed in the United States of America
ISBN: 978-0-578-45012-4
Library of Congress Control Number:

Written, Created and Designed by Sasha Gray

For Information, address:

Scattered Sasha
PO Box 118
Connelly Springs, NC, 28612
sasha@scatteredsasha.com

To all the Souls out there that struggle with life because you've forgotten something very important:

There's a whole lotta good in our souls, our hearts and our very being but we forget about it most of the time. We're way too busy tossing shame around like it's candy and hoping no one notices when we blow off a compliment or talk about ourselves like we aren't worthy of #allthethings.

You are so much more than any label, any past transgression, any opinion of someone else.

You are a magnificent creature placed in this universe to shine as the brightest star.

You are Unbreakable…..

Table of Contents

Introduction ... 1

Chapter 1
Bicycle Chains, Young Love, and Country Roads ... 3

Chapter 2
Taters, Bacon, and T-Shirts ... 13

Chapter 3
Buggies, Mad Dashes, and Parking Lots ... 25

Chapter 4
Feathers, Tiny Boxes, and Resurrections ... 37

Chapter 5
Silk Legs, Parties, and Complications ... 49

Chapter 6
Twisting, Turning, and Learning ... 59

Chapter 7
Date Nights, Photo Opps, and Perceptions ... 71

Chapter 8
Panic, Mayhem, and Detours ... 79

Chapter 9
Doors, Making a Scene, and Good Words ... 89

Chapter 10
Rocking, Rollin', and The Preacher 97

Chapter 11
Saggy Boobs, Bathtubs, and Treadmills 107

Chapter 12
Tractors, Nehi Sodas, and Larry 117

Chapter 13
Fried Chicken, Goals, and Crossing Yards 127

Chapter 14
Legos, Book Fairs, and Finding Joy 135

Chapter 15
Race Cars, Chances, and Fuel for your Fears 143

Chapter 16
One More Thing 151

Author Bio 155

Acknowledgments 157

Introduction

Hey Y'all....I'm so glad you're here.

I'm Sasha and my world is full on crazy town just about all the time, and every single day I feel like I just need to stop for a hot minute, call a friend, have lunch with my bestie, or chill out on the couch and catch up on whatever show I DVR'd last month.

But that doesn't happen very often. Usually it's a non-stop merry-go-round that speeds up right before it tosses you off and you roll around on the ground, gathering dust, dirt, and the detritus of life.

So, to try and wrap my head around some goodness every once in a while, I started writing stories.

These stories were woven with life lessons and along the way, I stopped long enough to realize life is what it is and nothing more. But we can choose to live it any way we want to.

And I chose to live it *happy*.

It just took me a while to figure it all out. But that's ok, too.

I also believe a few truths that have carried me through the daily grind....

I believe in kindness.
I believe in the power of the universe.
I believe chocolate and margaritas can solve a lot of problems.
I believe we're stronger than we realize.
I believe good words make a difference.
I believe in connections.
I believe in glitter, sparkling shiny souls, and goodness.

This book is part of my journey and I hope it will become part of your journey as well.

I included space to create your own life lessons, take from some of mine, or mesh the two together to make it work for you.

There's room for notes, doodles, and thoughts...because we always need a space to clear our hearts and heads and jot down something amazing that has been in our soul long enough.

The Mandalas you'll find after each chapter are just pretty...and if you're the type that likes to color, then you'll enjoy doing just that.

The stories in this book are all true and just a part of my daily life....you can usually find me with a sweet tea in one hand and a fan in the other, juggling the care of my 87-year-old daddy, a pre-teen full of drama, my traveling salesman of a husband, and one crazy dog.

And with a journey fraught with caffeine and chaos, and slapped together by pixie dust and tequila, I like to think I know a thing or two about life, building people up, creating laughter and spreading a little love....

Glitter & Grace, y'all!
Sasha

Chapter 1

Bicycle Chains, Young Love and Country Roads

When I was 13, my 'boyfriend' rode his bike 10 miles to see me for a 'date.'

And just to be clear, 'boyfriend' wasn't really what we called it back then. Nope, we were 'going together'.

My mama always said, "I don't know *where* you're going together, because you ain't dating until you're 16".

And since you can't drive at 13, even in the backwoods of North Carolina, my boyfriend decided to ride his trusty 10-speed the ten miles to see me.

Now, this wasn't 10 miles of nice, smooth, straight highway, complete with a bike lane, well marked turns, and new asphalt.

Nope, this was country road, complete with narrow lanes, no curbs, broken up pieces of road tossed aside from wrecks, daredevils and menacing teens, and enough curves to qualify as voluptuous.

When Chris* started out on that epic journey, he probably didn't know all these little details, but he decided to venture out anyway. See, he was from 'town' and I was from 'the country'. He lived on paved streets, with landscaped yards and sidewalks, neatly tucked behind fences and bordered by garages and neighbors.

I lived on 40 acres, with fields of corn and hay, the stray cow from the neighbor's dairy in my yard, and a dirt driveway that stretched a mile to the highway, hidden by tall trees planted by my daddy when he built our 'mansion on the hill'…which was really a ranch style house on the tallest part of the land, but no more a hilltop than a slight elevation in the earth.

Chris rode that bike for what I'm sure seemed like hours. I don't remember how long it took, only that he called from the phone hanging on the wall in his kitchen, to tell me he was on his way.

When he finally arrived, his pants leg was torn and there was dried blood on his leg. As a 13 year old awkward, gangly girl - full of drama, teen hormones, embarrassment and the built in sarcasm from generations of strong women - I'm sure I said something witty, and totally inappropriate, but I simply don't remember all the details.

What I do remember is that, along the way on this winding, narrow, country 2 lane black top, a dog ran out and attacked him, knocking him off his bike, tearing his pants and causing him to break the skin on his leg in the fall.

It wasn't a dog bite that got him, it was the chain on the bike. As it turns out, it was my uncle's dog, and I knew *exactly* where it had all occurred.

That particular stretch of road is Blue Hollow and it's notorious for wrecks, spirits and shenanigans. And the spirits are both the haunting kind and the liquid (*totally* for medicinal purposes) kind.

Even after the epic journey Chris took to see me, the trauma of the attack and the physical toil I'm sure it took, we still had fun. I remember trying to be cool and drinking my soda out of a straw (still in the local diner wrapper), and making fun of my mama's peanut butter on saltine crackers, because that was the thing to do.

He was still there when my Daddy got home from work, and he must have taken pity on the boy, because he loaded up his bike in his truck and drove the 10 miles to take him home.

We talked that night on the phone, our conversation full of long silences, nervous laughs and the dreams of teenaged years to come.

We broke up not too long after that….I think the difficulty of a long distance relationship was just too much, or it could have been our cultural differences….he with pavement, me with dirt….

Or it totally could have been that my uncle's dog tried to eat him and his parents said no more 10 mile epic bike rides out to the land of nowhere.

More likely, it was just that 13 year old learning curve into the world of semi adulthood, where you try to figure out what to do next, and how you're supposed to do it.

*name changed to protect the innocent

Life Lesson: You are worthy

I learned something that day that has stayed with me my entire life, and when you think about the fact that it's been more than 40 years since that fateful, day of my 13th summer, that's saying something.

I learned that people will surprise you if you let them, there really is good in the world, and young love is still as sweet as a perfect summer day.

It's pretty easy to get in the rut of not believing in yourself, and thinking you're not enough of anything. I hear it in voices camouflaged by pretense and hope, covering the truth with words that mean nothing when inside, the soul is breaking with heartache and pain.

The first step to believing in yourself is to start thinking it. That sounds simple enough, but often we think we have to go from a place of no self confidence to some giant leap frog step to runway fame and tv lights.

Because that seems like the only option.

It's not, and it doesn't even make sense. When you start thinking something, your brain does weird, science stuff (that's totally as technical as I can get...) that makes it so.

Ok, so it's not *quite that simple*, but for realz, y'all....your brain is a miracle worker.

Lemme break it down in steps (I do love me some steps and because it works for me, they'll have nice little boxes beside them so you can *check them off - Yasssssss!!*)

- ☐ Think: I am worthy. I am beautiful. I am enough of everything.
- ☐ Think: I deserve everything I want in life.
- ☐ Think: I am ready to receive all the goodness the universe has directed toward me.
- ☐ Think: I am worthy. I am beautiful. I am enough of everything.
- ☐ Say out loud: I am worthy.
- ☐ Say out loud: I am beautiful.
- ☐ Say out loud: I am enough of everything.
- ☐ Say out loud: I am ready to receive all the goodness the universe has directed toward me.

- ☐ Write it down: I am worthy.
- ☐ Write it down: I am beautiful.
- ☐ Write it down: I am enough of everything.
- ☐ Write it down: I am ready to receive all the goodness the universe has directed toward me.

The people that know such things say it takes 21 days to create a habit. I think it takes as much or as little time as it takes you to see there's been a change in your world and you like that change and want it to continue.

This whole 'think, say, write' process works because you are using your brain to retrain your thoughts. Thinking it, saying it, seeing it written….all these things are telling your brain the TRUTH.

And the truth is where it all begins.

Say it with me: I am worthy….I am beautiful….I am enough of everything.

Don't ever forget it….

Glitter & Grace,
Sasha

Life Guides

Use this guide to remind yourself of how amazing you really are!

List the ways you are enough....there are no rules, no right or wrong answers. How do you show up every day and be *more* than enough? Start by thinking it....

1. _____

   _____

2. _____

   _____

3. _____

   _____

4. _____

   _____

5. _____

   _____

Notes...Doodles...Thoughts on Life

I am worthy

Chapter 2

Taters, Bacon and t-shirts

I almost missed it....

If the light hadn't been red, I wouldn't have needed to slow down and would have just driven right by Jan's restaurant.

I caught a glimpse of the small sign just as it was almost out of eye sight, but that red light gave me a moment to consider what I had seen.

Built beside a small, tired convenience store with 2 gas pumps outside and a few potholes in the parking lot, it was a tiny place. Sandwiched between that convenience store and a closed barber shop, Jan's was bustling with business on a Tuesday at lunch.

Trucks with dirty wheels and fenders , SUVs with shiny coats of paint and work vans crowded into parking spaces without the benefit of lines and only beat up old railroad ties for a stopping point.

The Dollar General next door had warning signs that their parking spaces were only for Dollar General customers but that didn't seem to stop hungry patrons from parking in that lot and walking over to Jan's.

I was one of those rule breakers that parked next door and walked in...

Cobalt blue plastic booths, the tables sitting on posts driven into the laminate floor, were standing at attention, waiting to hold members of the community....a place where everyone knows your name and I heard choruses of "How's your daddy?" and "Think it's gonna rain some more?" echo off the walls and over the calls of "John! Your order's ready!".

The menu was a white board full of choices, placed in front of the fryer, grill and sandwich-making table, hiding employees that knew what you wanted before you made it to the counter. As soon as I walked in, two friendly young ladies in matching tie-dye shirts asked if they could help me, but I needed a minute to process, decide and breathe in the small town charm this place offered.

I decided on a bacon cheeseburger because...HELLO....Bacon. I was asked if I wanted a basket or just the sandwich and since I've always liked a basket, I decided to go all in and live on the edge. A basket it was.

"Fries or Tater Wedges?" came the reply.

And just over her shoulder, I could see this glorious pile of perfectly cooked tater wedges, just waiting for me to whisper the words that would allow me to see my plate piled high with the deliciousness I was sure would follow.

She jotted letters down on a menu pad, short hand acquired from years of doing this same thing, the same way for the same people.

BCB mayo was code for my Bacon Cheeseburger with only mayo and below those letters was just a "T".

"T" for Taters instead of "FF" for fries.

I knew I would love this place.

Tearing off the bottom of the menu pad, she handed me a small slip of paper with "46" in the corner, my ticket to lunch and anonymous new customer…I felt sure John didn't get a torn off ticket number, and neither did Miss Ruth or Charlie, both of whom came in after me and got their orders to go.

I sat down in a small 3 person booth (2 on 1 side, 1 on the other) and waited about 3 minutes for my number to be called, and when my small cardboard tray came out, with those golden tater wedges piled high and my bacon cheeseburger wrapped in slightly greasy wax paper, I didn't stop to think about anything other than how much I love diners, America, and small country towns….

As I ate (much faster and without any shame or concern about grease dripping off the corner of my mouth, spots of tater wedges dropped on the table or my almost untouched tea), I glanced around Jan's, and saw a community haven, where friends go to meet, nourish their souls and bellies and make sure a local landmark stays open.

The bulletin board with business cards, a flyer about a missing child, and a lost dog reward sheet was posted on the wall, filled with holes from abandoned notes, old cards long out of date and business and yard sales over since last summer. I'm guessing regulars rarely glanced at the board in the rush of lunch and dinner, but it's still there, in case anyone needs any of the services listed, just in case anyone finds a dog, or praise whomever you pray to, that baby girl that's missing.

There's a banner on the wall, proclaiming the year Jan's opened and that they've served the community for more than 35 years. That's history right there, as we watch retail and restaurants close every day, struggling to make it in a world that's surrounded by giant chains and fickle neighbors. But Jan's hangs on and hangs on tight, if the trucks, vans and cars outside in the parking lot on a Tuesday afternoon mean anything.

As I was getting up to get more tea, I walked by a man sitting in a booth, work boots covered in mud and work pants faded from years of wear. He was eating a burger, while another waited on his tray.

He asked: "What does your shirt say?"

I opened my sweater so he could read it….

"Mouth of a sailor, heart of a saint…my son is in the Navy and I saw 'Sailor' on there and wondered. My wife would really like that shirt…"

I thanked him and his son for his service, told him where I got it and hoped he remembered because I wanted his wife to have one, too.

After I sat back down, he continued his conversation with another man sitting 2 booths away, easy conversation about daddies, hospitals, mamas worrying and snow storms they didn't want to drive through.

As I finished my meal, I sat quietly and eavesdropped, hoping I wasn't obvious but it was easy as friends and neighbors chatted and shared life, making it easier to get through the tough times when you can tell someone else about your burdens.

Miss Ruth was frail but insisted she was fine when several asked….

Claire had broken her foot and had a cane, the doctor told her she'd need to be on it for a few more weeks….

The man sitting in the booth beside me had a daddy in the hospital, surgery happening soon….his daddy was getting a new heart valve and when he asked the doctor if it was, in fact, from a pig's heart the doctor told him that the one his daddy was getting was from a cow.

The man laughed with joy and delight as he told the sailor's father what his daddy said when he told him this…

"Daddy said, it'd better be from a bull!"

I left Jan's with laughter echoing in my ears from two friends that covered the worry life brings with humor, shared stories and lunch at a diner that brought the normal back every time they stepped through the door.....

Life Lesson: Soul-soothing is important

Life is so big, so overwhelming, and so messy that it's all we can do to get through each day sometimes.

The hustle and bustle of every day wears us down and helps us forget that we need our soul soothed, our mind calmed and our hearts given a burst of goodness so bright, we gotta wear shades.

I know how it is.....you give and give and give (and *give*) because THAT IS WHAT WE DO.

And, if push comes to shove, we don't mind it at all, because we do what we do for those we love.

Ok, sometimes we do what we do for people that are in our world because life happened, but still....we are doers.

So what happens when we run out of 'give'....what happens when our soul is empty, our mind is too full to think, and our hearts wait for direction that never comes because we simply cannot give anymore.

It's the proverbial 'out of gas' feeling that hits every single one of us when we don't stop to refill.

You've heard it before....the analogies are plentiful and the visuals they give make you nod your head, agree to everything being said, and the assurance (at least to yourself) that you *will* take the time you need, the space you need....the break you need.

Are you nodding your head right now?

Is your mind saying, "Oh yeah....I know what you are talking about!".

But we don't, because we don't think we *can*.

There's too much to do, too much on our plate, our calendar, our to-do list and our mind to fit *one more thing* in there, and certainly not something as trivial as *self-care*.

Self-care is the new buzzword around town, and all of a sudden, there are a whole lot of options surrounding us for ways to take care of that self that so desperately needs it.

There are spa days, girls trips, moms nights out, home parties, and weekends away.

And you're thinking....well SURE. I'm in, but .... who in the wild world of sports has the time, money or energy to do *any* of those things?

Let me offer you another option (or 4) that might work:

* Go for a drive
* Go for a walk
* Call a friend
* Eat ice cream for dinner

So....this seems odd, doesn't it? Go for a drive? Go for a walk? EAT ICE CREAM?

Here's the thinking behind these options....it's not the *thing* you do that refills your soul.

It's the time you take to do it.

All those awesome options for the girls night, weekends away, spa days, or whatever exist because everyone is trying to make the time you need to spend on yourself *worthy* enough for you to actually DO IT.

Of course you wouldn't just spend a weekend doing nothing simply to refill your soul, so the 'weekend getaway' has to be created so you'll feel like it's *something* you can go and do.

Let me propose a drastic change in thought: schedule 10 minutes a day to refill your soul.

And spend those 10 minutes however *you want to*.

Just enjoy them.

All 10 minutes.

All 600 seconds *just for you.*

Glitter & Grace,
Sasha

Life Guides

Use this guide to remind yourself of how amazing you really are!

List other ideas for soul-soothing things you can do....what fills you up and gives you the needed boost to get back to living your best life? Think WAY outside the box and write down anything that makes you smile. Then...when you schedule those 10 minutes each day, write down what you'll do during that time that's just for you.

1._____

_____

2._____

_____

3._____

_____

4._____

_____

5._____

_____

Notes...Doodles...Thoughts on Life

Find your Soul Soother

Chapter 3

Buggies, Mad Dashes, and Parking Lots

Well, we went to Walmart on the 3rd of the month because obviously I have to pay for the sins of a previous life, and my adventures began....

I pulled up on the concrete beside the pharmacy door, the one in as much of the middle of the giant Super Duper spend-all-day and all-your-money at once Walmart, careful not to block the road, the door or the random bus that was acting as a Blood Donor station AND the car with the logo all over it that was parked BEHIND it.

It was tricky, but I managed to slide right in, blinkers flashing and engine running as I dashed inside to get what I hoped was one of the electric chair buggy things.
In I dashed (Ok, I just sorta walked fast), face and hands cold in the 25 degree weather, but no worries...I was in a hurry and on IT.

First door, and no electric chair buggy things to be seen.

I looked hard, thinking perhaps these slightly-less-than-dining-chair size things could be hiding in the long row of regular buggies or behind the claw machine designed to steal quarters from unsuspecting children and their tired, exasperated parents, but nope!

No luck.

So I truck on in the store, walking really fast now, willing daddy to stay in the truck, the roving security guard not to see my totally illegally parked truck and the blood mobile not to need to move before I could get back.

I walked the length of the store, eyeing heads I spotted at elbow level, sizing up their carts to see how much more time they would spend in that rare, oh so precious electric chair buggy thing, hoping I could rush them with my Vulcan mind abilities, but they just kept cruising along.

I got to the other door, barely missing a mama and her 3 kiddos all lined up in a row, holding hands to stay together, but ... what a nice LINE it formed. I resisted the urge to sing "Red Rover, Red Rover, send Sasha right over" and kept heading to the OTHER electric chair buggy thing station.

Nope...none there.

So I power walked BACK to the other door I came in, willing someone to have finished shopping, parked their buggy and headed home to the ice cream I'm sure they were carrying to eat by the fireplace in their home.

It's possible I was slightly delusional by now, as I frantically searched for the elusive buggy thing...

Still none there.

I hit the exit door, which only opened about a foot. I don't know if you've ever seen me in person, but there's a LOT more of me than will fit through a sliver of a door opening...the cold must have gotten a hold of that door, because it was moving S-L-O-W and I had to slam on my boot covered brakes to keep from face planting into the thing, surely causing my search to be delayed.

The cold air hit my face at full blast, and my eyes watered slightly as I scanned the parking lot, looking for abandoned electric chair buggy things, lonely in the parking lot, pushed up on a sidewalk or even carrying someone to their car.

Hey, I'm not above 'helping' someone take their electric chair buggy thing BACK to the store!

And then...I saw the most beautiful thing...a man was riding one back to the outdoor department door!!

I heard the angels sing and the sky opened with karma flying overhead as I literally jogged (read: walked faster) past the random blood donor bus AND car, into the outdoor patio with bikes, and lawnmowers and sad, disregarded furniture waiting for the sun and warmer weather.

I breathlessly walked into the outdoor section of the store, saw the man that had ridden the electric chair buggy thing inside AND the chair itself!!

I grinned as I started to climb aboard and hit the trail.....and then an audible sigh left my soul as the man said, "It's dead, I couldn't even get it up to the front of the store. But there's some at the other entrance."
No.

No, my man who drives buggies, there's not.

I made my way back outside, momentarily considering grabbing a mini bike in a moment of desperation, but sanity reared up and snapped me out of my delusions....

I headed back toward the truck, past the blood donor bus AND car and started scanning the parking lot again.

I got back in the truck and told Daddy there were no electric chair buggy thin....BUTWAIT!

There...➢➢ RIGHT THERE between the Altima and the Subaru was the tobogganed head of a stranger gliding along, right about car door level and I KNEW he was riding an electric chair buggy thing!!

I told Daddy, perhaps a little more excitedly than I would normally be over such a find, that YES!! There was one...I just had to determine if he was riding it because HE needed it or he was bringing it back to the store.

I quickly got out of the truck, raced (read: walked quickly) into the store, and as the man was riding the electric chair buggy thing over to the regular buggies (ummm...maybe he was confused...), I started with:

"Sir! Sir! EXCUSE ME SIR!"

He stopped, turned to look at me, and just stared.

I prefer to think it was my captivating beauty and color coordinated hair and clothes that made him stare and not the look of a rabid animal running for its life in the woods after a zombie apocalypse, but hey, whatever...

"Sir, are you returning that?"

The nicest man I've ever met: Yes, someone just left it in the parking lot and I thought I'd bring it back.

Me: I'll take it from here, dude, OFF!

Ok, I didn't really say that, but I wanted to....

So I jumped on the electric chair buggy thing, slapped that puppy in reverse (it's just the other lever, there is no real satisfaction like you're changing gears and working the clutch, but go with me here...) and practically did a wheelie as I headed for the door and freedom, otherwise known as my truck with daddy securely inside, waiting to take Wal-Mart by storm.

Remember I told you about the door that was opening S-L-O-W-L-Y?

Yeah, well *I* forgot.

So I've got that bad boy going wide open, which is about 1/8 of a centimeter per hour, and I'm holding that lever all the way to the floor (handle, whatever...) and hunkering down, ready for that cold blast and my driving skills to take over.

I almost made it.

Like, I bet if there were only fractions of an inch LESS on either side of that fancy electric chair buggy thing, I would have cleared that door and been standing on the pedestal getting the gold.

Do you have any idea how hard those things hit when they've moving slower than a turtle on race day with a rabbit on its back?

Well, in case you don't, the answer is: Pretty dang hard!
Enough to bounce all of me around a little and (luckily) knock my hand OFF the pedal I was pushing to the metal (lever on the handle....whatever).

And THANK GOODNESS for that or I'd probably STILL be fighting with the door at Wal-Mart....

The door finally opened enough to let ALL of me AND the electric chair buggy thing OUT and I made a bee line for my truck, still where I left it, not towed, not empty, and not run over by a bus. I wheeled around the truck, and came up on Daddy's side, pulling as close as possible and slammed on the brakes (let go of the lever...whatever), ready to get this party started.

Daddy took one look at the electric chair buggy thing and said:
"That's not a Wal-Mart buggy. Did you steal that from someone....?"

Life Lesson: Perseverance is a virtue

Perseverance: the noun 'perseverance' is usually defined as steady persistence in the course of action, a purpose, a state, etc., especially in spite of difficulties, obstacles, or discouragement.

Well, don't *WE* have that in spades?

I believe the quote goes, "With perseverance, we can accomplish great things."

I totally agree.

I also agree we can accomplish great things just by walking through a door and choosing the right thing to say or do sometimes.

But perseverance shows us what we *can* do and reminds us that we are much stronger than we thought we were and that we've already come through some mighty big life lessons along our journey.

Looking back at accomplishments over the years, sometimes we can be amazed at what we went through to get to where we are now. I can remember looking at a completed project years after it was done, and still being quite proud of figuring out what to do, how to do it, and getting it done.

And when I am slapped with a brick wall these days, I know I am strong enough to break through it and smart enough to figure out a way around it.

The perseverance to get something done, get answers, figure things out and then make them happen (or decide to go in another direction) drives our spirit and reassures our soul that we are more than capable in so many areas of life.

It's just easy to forget when we focus on the big things instead of including the daily life affirming chores that make sure we survive another day.

So celebrate the perseverance in making your chaos normal and your life doable.

No one else can do it quite the way you do.

Glitter & Grace,
Sasha

Life Guides

Use this guide to remind yourself of how amazing you really are!

The little things in life make up the big things in life. Sometimes we forget that those little things are just as important as the others. Here, remind yourself of all that you do....list the small things in your world that help make the big things better.

1. _____

   _____

2. _____

   _____

3. _____

   _____

4. _____

   _____

5. _____

   _____

Notes...Doodles...Thoughts on Life

Patience is a virtue

Chapter 4

Feathers, Tiny Boxes, and Resurrection

My daddy needed a band-aid.

That's how it all started, this plunge into the abyss known as insecurity and doubt.

I brought the band aids back to the cabinet in the bathroom and, in the absence of a cheap box, all the headbands I never seem to wear anymore tumbled over into the empty band aid container and lay in a jumbled heap, all askew with dust, feathers, glittered rhinestones and faded satin staring at me in dismay.

I tried to pick them all up without putting the band aids down, but just managed to drop everything and cuss a little as headbands, first aid ointment, gauze pads (just in case) and extra large bandages (no name brands for us...generic will do just fine, thank you very much) fell to my feet in a heap.

After I put the band aids back where they belong, I gathered up the headbands, one by one and laid them on the counter, attempting to put some order in an unordered stack, hoping the next time (and there would be a next time) I needed something close by, they would stand straight and tall, waiting without falling.

The last headband I picked up was the one with a beautiful crown of gray, black, white and silver feathers layered on one side of a slim black metal band. I had gotten it in Nashville at Goorin Bros. Hat Shop, a too expensive piece of accessory, and a splurge of fast cash, squandered on something so frivolous I was hesitant to buy it at all.

But it was so stunningly beautiful, so soft and smooth to the touch and almost decadent in its luxury, I knew I had to have it and would wear it often. It matched my hair color and when I put it on my head, just past the front of my hair so it hovered behind my pouffy bangs, it offered a flash of whimsy, a touch of class and a whisper of fun.

When we got home from that trip, I put it with the other, lesser head bands, careful not to ruffle the feathers or get them too close to anything that would damage them.

That Friday, when we were getting ready to go out to dinner, I planned my outfit to match my new headband and gently placed it perfectly on my head, fixing my hair around the slim black metal so the feathers would all be showing.

I loved how I knew it looked ~ it looked exactly like me.

We chose a restaurant we had been to many, many times before and the waitress knew us well. As soon as we had seated ourselves, she came over with our drinks, not needing to ask what we wanted and said our appetizer was on the way.

And then she stopped, stared at my head for a moment, and said,

"What in the hell do you have on your head?"

It was that moment that I hesitated.

I doubted.

I questioned.

And I lost my love for that beautiful headband.

I stuttered that it was my new headband, reaching with unsure fingers to touch the feathers, thinking perhaps they had fallen off or turned an ugly rotting color during our travel time.

She said, "Well, I just don't like feathers on grown women. I think it looks stupid."

I was speechless, amazed and all the other words you can think of that you would be at that moment but simply stared, because really, what do you say at that point?

After we came home, agreed we needed to find a new place to eat and got ready for bed, I placed the headband back in the cabinet and didn't think about it much more, certainly not wearing it again. It became hidden in the clutter of life, feathers turning dusty and buried underneath things that didn't look stupid.

But tonight, as I smoothed my fingers over those feathers again, it brought back the excitement of my first glance at the headband, my first thought that I really could buy it AND wear it, and how glorious it would look in my hair. I could see me in the clothes I imagined it would match and caught a glimpse of me laughing as the feathers danced on my head.

And then, the memory surged forward from years ago, of ugly words, opinions of others that I let decide what I would do and wear. I recalled with amazing clarity the moment, where we were sitting, and the crisp clear voice of someone I really didn't even know destroying my joy.

At that moment, my brain tingled and tiny explosions of light bounced off the backs of my eyes as I felt this uprising begin, led by my mama looking down on me and cussing a little bit about not being here to snap me out of it.

Words and thoughts came together like fire and gasoline with all the moments of indecision in my life up to this moment tossed around and balled up, ready to spin out of control.

I KNEW I had a lot to say now, no stuttering speechless wonder at what the words would be.

Now I know ~ I am a grown woman. I have lived more than 55 years, birthed a child, raised children, married 2 men and loved a few more, lost a grown son, and gained others not born to me. I have bought homes, sold homes, lost homes and cars, been hired and fired and promoted and demoted. I have been slapped, attacked, accused and escaped. I have laughed, cried, sobbed and giggled, all uncontrollably. I have buried my mother, lost friends, and gained others that complete me. I have given pieces of my heart to some that needed the solace I could give. I have known heartache, loss, and grief so deep it shatters your soul into a million tiny pieces unable to be glued together again. I have experienced love, friendship, happiness, joy, kindness, and peace.

I am a survivor. I am unbreakable.
I love life and live it fabulously every single day.

I'm gonna wear that feathered headband any time I want to. I'll wear it to the grocery store, out to dinner, to the post office, and maybe even in the glitter dome when I work, because feathered headbands should never be hidden underneath anything and neither should you or I.

So I say to you: Wear your feathered headband….or whatever it is YOU want to wear. Yours might not be the exact same 'feathered headband' as mine, but don't let anyone else decide what makes you feel beautiful!

Life Lesson: Choose your own labels

Guess What?

People are going to call you names, tell you what you are and who you should (and shouldn't) be and smile while they're doing it.

They will freely toss labels at us like it's candy and we're supposed to gobble it up, say thank you and ask for more.

Those labels aren't who you are, and the people tossing them aren't label makers. But we sure let those labels land on us like the skin we're in, then we pat them down, rub them in and accept them for what they say.

When we allow someone else to label us as whatever they choose, we are giving others the power to decide who we are, and who we will become.

Because ultimately those labels won't be ones that are pretty, tied up in a bow and bestowed on us from a velvet pillow. Most often, those labels are shouted in anger, hurled in ignorance and slapped on with confusion.

And that's where it gets fuzzy. All those labels have some sort of toxic adhesive that just sucks the soul right out of us and when we bring those nasty things to the front of our soul, all the good stuff gets pushed to the side.

The Good Stuff just gets shoved out of our soul....it gets trampled on, it gets flown over, and shoved out of the way for this big, giant box that sits right in the middle of our gut that has the label "UGLY" on it.

The UGLY label is written in all caps, and red magic marker.

It's not even a pretty red. It's one of those orange-red-pink colors that doesn't even know what to call itself, so it settles for 'bittersweet' and suddenly you know *exactly* what color that is....

That big box of UGLY is sitting there in our gut...just waiting.

But....there's thousands of little boxes inside us. There's thousands of little boxes that surround that big box and those little boxes have "*love*" and "*happiness*" and "*friends*" and "*good person*" and "*good mother*" and "*kind*" and "*brave*" written on them, and they are surrounding this one giant box of ugly. Those are the labels YOU created for yourself.

But that big box of ugly is sitting right in the middle.

Maybe it says "worthless".
Maybe it says "stupid".
Maybe it says, "fat".

Whatever it says, whatever your box is full of, whatever labels have been hurled at you from others that you let sit there on your skin and *in that box*, by allowing that big box of "ugly" to take up space in our soul, we discredit all those little tiny boxes surrounding it that say the good things.

Now why is that big box of ugly more important than those little boxes of all the good?

Here's the thing, y'all....That big box labeled "ugly" was the exact same size as all those little boxes of good things. We just inflated it. We gave it much more power, much more stuffing, much more size than all the little boxes.

We need to gather all the little boxes, those little boxes labeled with "*love*" and "*happiness*" and "*friends*" and "*good person*" and "*good mother*" and "*kind*" and "*brave*" that are there inside us and inflate those as well.

They need to jump on that big old box of ugly and kick it out and let me just tell you, if I could reach down in your gut, (which wouldn't be really a pleasant thing for either of us), but if I could just reach down in your gut and grab that big old box of ugly out and crumple it up, stomp on it, run over it with my truck, spit on it, toss it in the burn pit and burn it, and kiss it goodbye, I would.

But I can't. Unfortunately, neither can anybody else.

That's all on you my friend.

You have to take that big box of ugly and take care of it yourself. You can take it out, you can stomp on it, spit on it, run over it with your truck, give it to the dogs to tear apart, burn it, and kiss it goodbye.

But that big box of ugly? It's got to go. You have to fill up those little tiny boxes with all the stuff that you know you are. Because here's the thing, you and others have been reading those other labels....and you've begun to believe them.

And those little boxes? We're going to FILL THEM UP with the good. And then they'll crush down the giant box of Ugly. They will smother it out and it will be able to be yanked out of your soul, run over with the truck, spit on, burn, eaten by the dogs, and kissed goodbye because there won't be room for it.

Then when someone tosses a label and it lands on you, the only thing you'll remember are the thousands of little boxes and all the labels on each one. And you get to decide what to do with the newest label... toss it, keep it, change the words or ignore it. It's up to you.

Because you are, in fact, the label maker for *you*.

Glitter & Grace,
Sasha

Life Guides

Use this guide to remind yourself of how amazing you really are!

What are the labels you *want* on your soul? This guide has 10 lines but you can add as many as you want...remember the 1000 boxes inside your soul? Yep....they all are filled with good things. Think about the ones you want to have front and center every single day and write those down so you'll be sure and remember them when someone tosses a new label your way.

1._____

2._____

3._____

4._____

5._____

6._____

7._____

8._____

9._____

10._____

Notes... Doodles... Thoughts on Life

Choose your own label

Chapter 5

Silk Legs, Parties, and Complications

Semi Formal should be black velvet yoga pants....

For the first time in several years, my husband's company decided to have a Christmas Party. Sounded good to me...food, drinks, and maybe a little entertainment.

And then I saw the actual invitation and those dreaded words appeared like tiny reindeer on Christmas Eve:

Semi-formal attire

Did we REALLY want to go?

I decided to look up 'semi-formal attire' just to make sure I hadn't forgotten what that meant, since it had been years since I'd worn anything other than jeans, yoga pants and long skirts.
Turns out 'semi-formal attire' is VERY specific.

Velvet, satin, silk, 'good' polyester (there are good and bad polyesters??? Who knew?).

I dug around in my closet and found a 'little black dress' I wore on a cruise about 6 years ago and with a little help from Spanx, pantyhose small breaths, and a lot of standing, I felt sure I'd be able to wear it just fine.

I bought the pantyhose in the egg and double-checked the size...yep, all those grid marks told me was that a giant range of people could fit this size and I was lucky enough to be one of them.

By the way...they lie.

The evening arrived, along with questionable decision-making. I got ready and began to get dressed, thinking I had better hurry up if I wanted to make sure I wasn't naked when the babysitter arrived.

I sat down and pulled the golden silk from the egg, slightly excited that my legs would be all soft, and silky skinned, if only for a few hours.

I was careful not to snag the precious nylons on toenails or rough heels, maneuvering slowly over each as I pulled the first leg up to my knee.

Bending over in the chair for that long was a little tiring, but I knew I had to get the other leg on so I pushed on and kept bending. I managed to get the 2nd leg covered and the hose pulled up to my knee as well, but this is where things get ugly.

As I gently pulled the hose up and over my knees, I realized things weren't quite like they should be.

As a matter of fact, things completely stopped as I got to my thighs.

Seems the hose were completely twisted, even though I was so very careful to keep them straight.

There was a line of nylon threatening to cut all circulation off my right leg, wrapped tighter than Dick's hatband (who the heck is Dick, anyway?), and not budging at all. It made an indention, actually cutting into my thigh and I began to worry I might pass out if I didn't quickly remove the offending nylon.

About this time, Mac walks in the bedroom and gives me a strange look. I might have appeared slightly haggard and a little sweaty. My makeup might have been 'glistening'....I MIGHT have looked at him and said something along the lines of, "Why don't YOU put on pantyhose sometimes and see how it feels!!" at a slightly louder than normal speech tone.

He mumbled something foolish about being sure those pantyhose weren't meant to do that and decided it was in his best interest to leave the bedroom until I was ready.

So I began to disengage the tourniquet that wrapped around my leg, and in doing so, managed to get the entire pair of pantyhose stuck somewhere between my thighs and above my knees, with the crotch just out of reach.

If I reached around my backside, I couldn't reach the center to pull them up, and if I bent over frontward to pull them up, I was only able to pull up part of them.

I wondered at that point if yoga pants were considered 'semi-formal' in any culture in the world and if I had time to look that information up and study enough to pass myself off as a resident of whatever culture that was before we left.

I made one final gesture to pull them up, leaning forward and pulling with both hands, jerking hard enough to hear to all to familiar rip of nylon tearing and a run beginning from the toe and continuing to the knee.

Which made it MUCH easier to just tear them off and throw them away!

Luckily I had an old pair of tights, light enough to pass as 'in an emergency' and lemme tell ya, THIS was an emergency! I pulled them on, slipped on my dress and said a small prayer that they'd last until at least dessert.

The story should end there, but it didn't.....I partook of the wine and Mac had a few beers.

When the company photographer came around to each table to take pictures, I politely held my glass in front of my face, while Mac grabbed his glass and proceeded to slug back whatever remnants remained.

When our table mate asked why I didn't want to show my face, my slightly evil sarcastic side emerged and I said, "Oh I don't want his wife to know I'm here!"

I totally blame it on the pantyhose.

Life Lesson: Don't always follow the rules

I'm a rule follower.

I'm a rule breaker.

I'm complicated.

I want to follow the rules, respect what they stand for and the people who came before me, creating whatever rules they created and making sure they were laid out for all to see, know and follow.

But the other part of me (I like to call her Veronica) likes to shake things up, raise a little hell, and thumb my nose at *all* the rules without a second thought as to why they were created, who created them or *if* I should follow them.

So yeah...it's a little bit complicated over here.

I like to think there's a narrow path that both sides of the line can follow, weaving back and forth like a drunken elf, hopping on and off the line, tip toeing along and giggling when things get a little ... 'complicated'.

When we follow the rules blindly, and I'm speaking of *'all the rules'*....you know...of LIFE....and never question where they came from, who created them or even if they are the *ones* for us, then we're just floating along forgetting that we get to make the decisions about our journey.

And lemme tell ya....making my *own* decisions is Huge to me.

Like Vivian at the Dress Shop on Rodeo Drive Huge.

But it's also pretty danged scary.

So we continue on down the road, someone else's rules guiding us along the way, never realizing that we don't always have to follow *all* the rules, and we can create our own ones, too.

How can we recognize, then change, the rules we don't want (or need) in our lives?

Here are some options:

- ☐ Define the 'rules' you live by....anything with 'always' or 'never' as the beginning is generally a 'rule'.
- ☐ Decide if each one was your rule or handed to you by someone else.
- ☐ Decide if this rule is a benefit or a hinderance to daily life.

- ☐ Decide if this rule can be modified, or should be tossed completely.
- ☐ Create your "Rules to Live By" (Hint: Guess what the Life Guides will be!)
- ☐ Revisit every year.

Is this something you can do while you're doing 27 other things and life is crazier than usual?

Probably not.

Is this something you can do on a Sunday afternoon or whenever life is calmer and you can think straight for 2 minutes without being interrupted 12 times?

Yes.

This is also an on-going action....you'll be handed new rules all the time.

It's up to you to decide if you're a rule follower or a rule breaker on each one!

Glitter & Grace,
Sasha

Life Guides

Use this guide to remind yourself of how amazing you really are!

Rule to Live By ~ Start with 5....the rest will come. Write in pencil because you'll want to change them along the way. Create a new list anytime you need to and remember...your journey ~ your map!

1. _____

   _____

2. _____

   _____

3. _____

   _____

4. _____

   _____

5. _____

   _____

Notes... Doodles... Thoughts on Life

Don't always follow the rules

Chapter 6

Twisting, Turning, and Learning

Just as a point of reference, I would be considered a 'big busted woman'. The actual size is irrelevant, but the story makes *much* more sense if you know this bit of info. And now...the *rest* of the story.

On the eve of my shoulder surgery, it occurred to me that I wouldn't be able to wear a bra and the likelihood of going out in public during my recovery was high. I didn't want to receive pity looks from people because I grew boobs in my stomach, so I rushed to the Internet to purchase a strapless bra. I chose the prettier of the 2 strapless choices in my size that JC Penney had on line. It arrived a few days later and when the weekend arrived, I chose to tackle this newly discovered chore of dressing.

I only had the use of one arm, but I showered and dried off, a feat within itself. I got the pretty, clean bra and slung it around my body with the hooks in front, of course. I managed to hook all 5 of the hooks in the middle selection and then proceeded to attempt to slide it around so the hooks would be in the back and the cups in the front.

Now, by this time, I was slightly damp from perspiration because of the effort I'd exerted so far.

So sliding wasn't exactly easy. As a matter of fact, the SOB would hardly move at all. I have to rest with the hooks and cups on my sides, hoping I'll not have to go out in public like this, which would actually be worse than having boobs in your stomach.

Finally I got it in the correct place, but the back is very low from all that wiggling and moving around, so it appears to be a halter back bra.

As I looked in the mirror, I realized why it hasn't moved much at all.

To be able to support all that weight without straps, they were required to put as much wire and as many seams in the bra as possible. It looks like a freakin' glider plane with the wings directly under my arms.

It was actually standing on it's own and I bet if I didn't have it on, it would still stand on it's own.

So after this realization, I tried to move it around a bit, fitting things where they should go. I then realized it's too loose and isn't as comfy as I had hoped. I began to move it back around to change the hooks.

After only 10 minutes of moving, wiggling, tugging and pulling, I managed to get the bra back around with the hooks in the front and the cups in the back. I re-hooked the hooks in the tightest position, so it will be good and snug because I surely wouldn't want it falling down now.

I turned and turned and turned and pulled and pulled and pulled and tugged some more and finally got the parts where they should be.

Again, the back is very low but I figure I'll just go with it at this point, maybe I'll wear something backless.

So I began the process of getting things in the proper place in front. I jiggled, shrugged and moved around until the cups appear to be in the proper place.

Now it's time to check things out and see how it looks.

Have Mercy, y'all…. there's enough white material on my front to cover several small children. The bra is actually not touching the front of my body in any place except directly under my boobs where the wires are pretending to be covered.

And in reality, the bottom of the bra is about mid-way down my stomach, curling up in ugly bunches in various places. So I tried to turn down all the pieces of material I can reach with one arm.

Finally, in exasperation, I think, "The hell with it, the ones in back won't be noticed…. I'll ditch the backless idea anyway".

Now, I have the bra in place to the best of my ability. It's standing at attention on my front with the wings prepared to take flight under my arms. I guess that's to take care of any roving breast you might have on your sides.

I look online again to see what I ordered for future reference, but I have now sworn off of any surgeries for the rest of my life.

Get this, it's a MINIMIZER!

Maybe if you were an elephant.

I get dressed, another effort, but I've chosen a button up sweater, much easier than anything else. As a matter of fact, I'd just been able to dress myself 4 days after surgery, *if* it's a button up top.

So, I have this sweater on, and it's sticking out in front with a life of it's own, but I figure that's the better of the 2 options.

I go run some errands. I made it home and *I am exhausted.*

Thinking I will need to rest up for life duties like breathing and sitting upright, I crashed for a short 2-hour nap.

When I awoke with a shortness of breath, I realized there was this vise on my chest…no, wait, I've fallen asleep with my bra on!!

I got up, somewhat light headed and attempted to get the bra off.

No such luck. It's stuck like glue. I'm really glad I fastened it tighter now.

I tugged, rested, tugged, rested and finally gave up. Maybe if I sat real still the wires wouldn't cut off my circulation and I'd be able to breathe.

Maybe my husband would come home early.

At 6:00 pm, I heard the door open so I rushed to the door with my back turned and my shirt up yelling, "take it off, take it off".

My husband grinned and thought, "Okkkaaaayyyyyy".

Bless his heart….

He unhooked the bra and gets it off.

I let out a huge breathe of relief, gave him the bra and told him to enjoy himself, I'm sure the bra could hold its own.

Life Lesson: Plan ahead

I'm a planner.

It's in my DNA like brown eyes, thick hips, and skinny lips. I could no more change my need to plan *every little thing* than I could change my height.

Yet, there I was....without a plan in sight for a surgery I *had* planned for months.

I get too much grief from others that suggest I should be more spontaneous, live more 'in the moment', not be so 'rigid'.

But I'm not buying into that thought process because planning is *in my soul* and I'm just fine with how my process happens.

By planning out the little things, the big things flow much easier and I'm all about things flowing along as easily as possible. After all, making life easier (and better) is often my goal!

So a-planning I shall go.

Now, what makes planning your day-to-day activities and life *better* than flying by the seat of your pants, grabbing onto the rail of the caboose with your pinky and hoping the curves ahead don't toss you off the cliff?

I'm pretty sure the answer is in that visual…

Does this mean you need to spend hours or even longer on creating a detailed plan to micromanage each part of your day.

Not even a little bit.

It can be as simple as jotting down your ta-da list (SO much better than a to-do list, don't you think?) on a napkin, or as detailed as a spread sheet, app, or work book.

Whatever *works* for you is what's most important.

And if you're thinking that this is just the *most ridiculous* thing ever, because you don't need help navigating the chaos and crazy, then *that is fabulous*.

But, if you're thinking you could always use a new idea, a tip that works or some thoughts you hadn't had yet, then let's dive right in!

Here's a few ideas to get started:

- ❐ Meal planning ~ and that doesn't have to be a month of meals, recipes, and ingredients. It can simply help to have an idea sheet of meals your family likes, and that can be made in 30 minutes.
- ❐ Emergencies ~ that list of people to contact when something happens....you won't need the stress of trying to remember *who* to call when you're in panic mode.
- ❐ Personal info ~ Do you or any of your family take any medicine on a regular basis? My husband travels, and I know his info, but I know for a fact that he has no idea about my day-to-day life, simply because he's not present. Having medical information, medicines, even my doctor's name and number in a nice file he can get to makes sure *I* get the care I need and he isn't guessing all the good stuff.
- ❐ Electronic Info ~ If you lost your wallet, would you know the credit cards that were in there, and the number to call to cancel them. I can tell you that we didn't when Mac lost his wallet on a business trip. We panicked....and it took the credit card company calling to question a charge before we remembered them all. So...copy those bad boys, put them somewhere safe and feel better!
- ❐ Family ~ Does everyone that needs to know, know the procedure with your family members? If you have school age children, the schools usually do a good job of collecting info but if something

were to happen to you, is there a plan in place for even picking them up and knowing what to do?

Now that you've read through this list, does it make a little more sense to have a plan for certain areas of your life?

Wouldn't it make an already stressful time *less stressful* to have these plans in place and give you that always needed peace of mind?

It does for me....and I'm gonna bet it does for you, too!

Glitter & Grace,
Sasha

Life Guides

Use this guide to remind yourself of how amazing you really are!

What could you make a plan for that would make your life easier? Jot down some ideas, create a list and just get started. That's the hardest part!

1. _____

   _____

2. _____

   _____

3. _____

   _____

4. _____

   _____

5. _____

   _____

Notes...Doodles...Thoughts on Life

Plan Ahead

Chapter 7

Date Nights, Photo Opps, and Perceptions

As people sometimes do, my husband and I recently went to the grocery store. And because we like living on the edge and that's what we do on date nights. Annndddd because we never have date nights and didn't know what *else* to do since we were out of milk, soup and eggs.

We were trying to be efficient...Mac and I both had the list on our handy dandy phone app, so we could divide and conquer....which actually means he'd look at all the wine and beer, finally choose something, then meander over to the meat section while I cruised the rest of the store and checked things off the list.

I was looking at the lunch meat and Mac was across the aisle looking at the steaks. (This is the story of my life....lunch meat and steaks divided by a section of cold areas and linoleum.)

He beckoned me over (not like in Pretty Woman or anything....not that gentle wave and whistle that makes you smile...more like, "Hey, you gotta see this" yelled across the heads of 4 people pushing buggies while they looked for the perfect pack of bacon or hotdogs...).

I wheeled around, narrowly missing a man browsing the BOGO chicken legs and rolled up beside Mac, fully expecting him to put something in the buggy.

I sure didn't need to see any raw meat, I totally prefer to see it cooked and then it's a little iffy.

He tried to hand me a package of something, but I was having none of it. Actually, I wasn't even looking his way, instead gazing at the creamer container just ahead, mentally calculating how many bottles I'd need for the next few weeks and wondering if they had the "Light" Caramel Macchiato.

He nudged my arm and said....."Photo opp..."

(I'll have to talk later about how this proves to me once again that he truly does 'get it' and knows a good story when he sees one, but that's a whole 'nuther story...)

As I glanced down at what his hand was holding, I smiled all over the place.

Then we laughed and laughed and giggled some more like high school kids that found something risque and no one else knew anything about it.

Mac finally stopped laughing long enough to say...."Wonder what would happen if we mixed The Greek God and The Stout Sexual Chocolate Beer Bratwurst together" and we doubled over with laughter once again.

I'm reminded of times people have asked where I get my stories and if everything I tell is "Really" real....and I just have to say, "*how* could I even make this stuff up???"

And then there's the part of the trip where I got the fringe of my ankle length sweater caught in the wheel of the buggy but that story will have to wait, too...

Life Lesson: laugh out loud often

As children, we laugh without inhibition, without fear of what people might think of us, or what we might appear to be....crazy, messy, or too much of anything.

Somewhere along the line of becoming an adult, we lose that inhibition and become very concerned about what people might think of us, what we might appear to be, and how we are perceived.

Ain't *that* a shame.

There's a lot of science behind how laughter affects us, proven with words written by people smarter than me:

> *"Laughter decreases stress hormones and increases immune cells and infection-fighting antibodies, thus improving your resistance to disease. Laughter triggers the release of endorphins, the body's natural feel-good chemicals. Endorphins promote an overall sense of well-being and can even temporarily relieve pain."*

Now I don't know about you, but *anything* that can promote an overall sense of well-being and temporarily receive pain is a winner in my book.

And **laughter** can do BOTH those things

So now let's talk about being concerned about how you appear to others, how they perceive you and what they might think about you when you laugh out loud.

The only words we need to say are....

WHO CARES!!!!

I'd like to issue you a challenge....the next time you find something funny, see something that brings a smile to your face, or laughter erupts from your soul.....take it to the next level.

Laugh out loud.
Laugh as long as you can.
Laugh as *often* as possible.

And feel better just by doing so!

Glitter & Grace,
Sasha

Life Guides

Use this guide to remind yourself of how amazing you really are!

What makes you laugh? It's a very personal thing...for example, my husband loves slap stick comedy but that's just not my thing. I prefer quick-witted, fast paced, sarcastic conversations to get my giggle on! Here, list your favorite funny movies...think about the scenes that make you laugh and then *practice* laughing out loud. Sounds crazy doesn't it....but really, practicing something you want to change is where you begin.

1. _____

   _____

2. _____

   _____

3. _____

   _____

4. _____

   _____

5. _____

   _____

Notes...Doodles...Thoughts on Life

Laugh out loud often

Chapter 8

Panic, Mayhem, and Detours

I was driving along, minding my own business, even sorta paying attention to the world around me. Nary a cell phone was in sight. Let me set this up for you:

The road was 2 lanes and there were several cars behind a 'chicken truck' and I was one of those several cars. (Just in case you're unclear as to what a 'chicken truck' is, it's a tractor-trailer/semi flatbed carrying crates/cartons/cases of live chickens.) The road was changing to 4 lanes just up ahead and we were all anxious to pass the chicken truck.

IF YOU HAVE A WEAK STOMACH, ARE VERY SENSITIVE OR ARE EATING WHILE YOU ARE READING THIS
STOP NOW!!!<<<<<
YOU HAVE BEEN WARNED!!!

As soon as the road changed to 4 lanes, we all began passing the chicken truck. There was a stop light ahead and **we** all saw the red light, but apparently the truck driver did not. The car in front of me stopped at the red light and so did I.

The trucker was in the left lane and didn't see the light until it was almost too late. He slammed on his brakes and stopped just past the white line. When he did that...everything jostled in the back of the truck....and I mean EVERYTHING.

Apparently, the crates that were holding some of the chickens weren't latched very well at all. So when the truck came to a full stop at the stop light, the chickens said, "HEY - Lookee here! We can GET OUT!"

And Get OUT they did! They hopped down, flew a little, landed on the bed of the truck and on the road.

Now, I need to tell you that the guy driving the little Honda in front of me was blowing the horn, waving his arms, yelling ~ doing all the things he could do to get the attention of the truck driver before the light changed to green.

Me?
I was trying to move my truck a little bit to the right so the two chickens that were right at my wheels wouldn't get crushed when I moved.

The driver didn't see anything. He DID NOT SEE live chickens flying all over the road, landing on the bed of the truck, falling to the road, hanging out all over cars or the general disarray that was about to take place.

The light turned green. The driver drove. Chickens didn't make it.

PEOPLE WERE GOING CRAZY!!!

Cars were diving off the road, more chickens were flying off the truck, hitting cars and the road and anything else in their path.

Well, I couldn't just let this continue because now I'M the one right behind the truck.

So I do what any woman alone in this kind of situation would do:

I called 911.

"911-what is your emergency?"

Me: "There's chickens all over the road!!!!!!!"

"Ma'am, is this a fire or medical emergency?"

Me: "I DON'T KNOW...THERE IS THIS CHICKEN TRUCK AND THE LATCH TO THE CHICKEN COOP-THINGYS ARE UNHOOKED AND THERE ARE CHICKENS FLYING OUT OF THE TRUCK GOING EVERYWHERE. PEOPLE ARE RUNNING OFF THE ROAD, TRYING TO MISS THE FLYING CHICKENS AND THEY ARE D.Y.I.N.G. ALL OVER THE PLACE"

"Yes Ma'am. Where are you now?"

Me: "On a bridge". (I think he wanted more info....)

"Ma'am, what bridge?"

Me: "ummmm, I'm not sure..hang on....Oh Shit, there's another one....I Gooottttaaaa miss it....Oh, sorry about that. The Shit part I mean. Ok, I'm on Hwy 115"

"North or South?"

Me: "Huh? I just crossed the bridge before the fire department....OH WAIT, he's turning, he's turning. He's turning....into the road to the chicken plant. Oh GOOD! You can get him! CALL THEM NOW!!!"

"Yes Ma'am, we'll call the chicken plant now. Thank you ma'am."

Now, I am TORN UP about all this and have to pull over and rest a little bit before I get where I'm going.

My next thought is to what happened when the driver pulled up to the gate at the Chicken Plant....

"Ah, Norm (apologies to all the people named Norm out there....), you seem to be missing a few chickens....."

Norm: "What are you talking about? Don't you think I would notice if I was missing a few chickens?"

No Norm, I do not think you'd notice at all.

Life Lesson: Know what's behind you

There are a lot of great messages that talk about not looking back because you're not going that way.

I agree that you need to keep your eyes, dreams and goals focused on what's ahead of you, because you really can't do anything to change the past....

However....

We have to bring the person we have become along with us on this journey.

We can't leave her at the starting gate...
We can't leave her at a detour...
We have to bring her along...

That way she'll be able to help navigate those curvy roads, those detours, those lefts, those rights, and those construction zones.

Because she will have had those experiences and help guide us on this journey. She'll be the one that points you in the right direction, the one that nudges you when you need to think again and the one that reminds you how far you've come so you can continue on.

Our past has a funny way of playing a giant part in our future and when we toss it away like a bad piece of fruit in the bottom of the basket, we discount and discredit the experience, often forgetting the valuable lessons we learned, leaving us open to make them again.

Bring your history in to the present....let it simmer beside your dreams, hopes, and goals and watch the two mesh together, rising out of the murky water of indecision, bringing you to easier decisions based on *you and what you've already been through, accomplished, and conquered.*

Glitter & Grace,
Sasha

Life Guides

Use this guide to remind yourself of how amazing you really are!

Your past holds your hand along the journey to your future. Write down 5 experiences that could help guide you to your hopes, dreams, and goals!

1._____

_____

2._____

_____

3._____

_____

4._____

_____

5._____

_____

Notes...Doodles...Thoughts on Life

Know what's behind you

Chapter 9

Doors, Making a Scene, and Good Words

The only electric wheelchair with a buggy at Walmart was on the other side of the store from where we parked.

I left daddy in the truck while I searched and when I found it, the only real option was to drive that sucker out the door, down the sidewalk, across the roadway and over to my truck.

I had unplugged the chair to hit the road but I'm not sure it was fully charged .... it was barely rolling and at one point, I was thinking about asking for a tow but I didn't see any electric wheelchair buggy pulling people around.

So I rolled on .... like a turtle going uphill through molasses.

And when I left the truck, daddy was sitting inside, impatiently waiting.

Obviously I was gone too long...

By the time me and ol' blue made it back to the truck, daddy was standing outside the door, hanging on for dear life and cussing my back seat where I had conveniently put his walker.

And when I saw this emergency in the making, I started yelling at him to STAAAAPPPPPP right there and Donotfortheloveoftacos move AT ALL.

Now I want you to picture this scene...

A purple and silver haired fluffy woman riding a pathetically slow electric wheelchair (with a buggy attached thankyouverymuch), rolling across the Walmart parking lot, gunning the bright yellow handlebar throttle, leaning as far forward as possible (surely that would make it go faster), yelling STAAAPPPPP in the direction of an 87 year old shaky man hanging onto a dirty Suzuki SUV door.

Nothing to see here, folks, just keep moving ....

And just so ya know, I made it to the truck before he fell, and we trudged onward with our adventures!

It's the little things, y'all....

Life Lesson: You can't control others

One of my very favorite quotes is: You can't control how others act. You can only control how you *re*-act.

THIS...this has been a mantra for many of my years.

But before those years showed up....well, let's just say it *wasn't* my mantra.

Nope, I'd get madder than a hornet that had been swatted on one side, and then I'd start yelling, flailing my arms all over the place, stomping and making *everyone* around me ever so *slightly* uncomfortable.

The moment I saw an *adult* flinch because of my actions, it was like a slap to the face followed by a giant bucket of very cold water.

I realized I needed to stop letting everyone else 'get' to me. I had to find a way to control my emotions, calm the hissy fits down, and let that shizzle go.

I used empathy, positive affirmations, meditation, and sometimes a margarita to get me there. There was a lot of starts and stops and starts again. Often, I'd come back to the realization long after the emotions had taken over, slammed me down and run over me with a truck.

Lessons can really be hard sometimes....

I can still get mad, throw a (much smaller) hissy fit, and realize I've let someone else's actions dictate how I act, but I'm much quicker to remind myself of ways to get *out* of that space.

Here's a list of suggestions if you'd like to change the way you *re*-act:

- ☐ Listen to your words. Do you hear what you're saying, and can you rationalize the meaning? If it's doing more harm *to you* than good, then stop the second you realize it.
- ☐ Listen to what someone else is saying. Does it really impact you? Do you really have to comment, get involved, have your say, or the last word? If any of those answers are 'no', then walk away.
- ☐ Realize the desire to want others to be like you is impossible to achieve (and really...we don't want *anyone* else to be like us!). I believe most reactions from others' actions happen because we simply can't fathom how someone else could act/speak/believe the way they do.

- When something someone is doing or saying is bothering you, close your eyes and focus on something else for a couple of minutes (ok, DON'T do this if you're driving….). The brain can*not* focus on 2 things at the exact same time, so you'll be 'taken away' (Calgon, anyone?) from the visual and the audio and it won't be in your mind for at least those few minutes. When you open your eyes, you will be more focused and calm, and better able to deal with the issue.
- Find the positive words, affirmations, quotes, voodoo, juju, or curse words that calm your brain and write them EVERYWHERE you can so you'll see the often. Read them, repeat them, memorize them and *use* them.
- Remember that *you are the one in control of how you react….*

The biggest part of changing a habit is beginning the new action you want to replace it with. It doesn't happen overnight, or immediately or even sometimes after lots of practice and training.

But if you are willing, and the want to change is bigger than the current habit, you will get there.

I know you can do it…

Glitter & Grace,
Sasha

Life Guides

Use this guide to remind yourself of how amazing you really are!

Good words make a difference, and I'm here to prove it. Jot down 5 quotes, phrases, affirmations, juju, or whatever soothes your soul when you read or hear them.

1. _____

   _____

2. _____

   _____

3. _____

   _____

4. _____

   _____

5. _____

   _____

Notes...Doodles...Thoughts on Life

You can't control others

Chapter 10

Rocking, Rolling and the Preacher

It sounded like a good idea at the time....

Tater wanted to ride her bike, and since it's only 91 degrees instead of 101, and there looked to be a storm a'brewin, I said, "Sure....but let's go over to the church parking lot."

I had already started thinking about all the details, because I'm a detail girl and even though this APPEARED to be just a girl riding her bike in a parking lot, there was SO much more to consider....

1. It's hotter than the gates of Hell (the fact that we were headed to church when I thought that isn't lost on me).
2. With a storm coming, the chances of us ~~having to suffer through~~ being able to enjoy a long stay would be (mercifully) short.
3. The church had their parking lot repaved 2 weeks ago and all that smooth asphalt was perfect for bike-riding, but not so good for spectating.

We walked to the garage and as I raised the garage door for her to get the bike, I wondered when I had last seen my camp chair ~ those wonderous folding chairs that come with their own sleeping bag ~ and if, in fact, I still had one.

After a quick glance around the garage, I saw no camp chair, but I DID see the perfect solution: An office chair, holding space until I could get it upstairs to the Glitter Dome (otherwise known as my office).

I looked out the garage door at the church parking lot, clearly visible across our yard, through the gravel driveway, and past some bushes.

No Problem!

I could easily ROLL that office chair over to the parking lot, park it in the shade and watch that baby girl ride to her heart's content.

Or until the rain rolled in, whichever came first.

Right there, I shoulda backed up and thought through that process, but I kept pushing on.

And just in case you're wondering, office chairs aren't really meant to go off-road.

But I persevered, half pushing, half dragging and even resorting to carrying that dang chair over the roughest parts of the journey. Every now and then, Tater would turn around, look at me and say, "Are you coming?"
Yes child, I'm coming. And so is my chair.

We finally made it to the church parking lot, and I parked me and my chair under the thankyoubabyjesus for the tree with shade.

And THAT'S when the trouble started.

Just about the time Tater made one circle over that smooth as silk new asphalt, a car turned in and pulled up right in front of my chair. I was *all* ready to go all Sasha-bear on whoever it was DRIVING where my baby girl was riding her bike!

Turns out it was the preacher.

Now, here's the thing: I've never met the preacher whose church backs up to our property, through the yard, over the gravel driveway and past the bushes.

Nope, he pretty much stays over at his place on Sundays and Wednesdays and I pretty much stay over at my place. But on that hot Saturday afternoon, we came to know each other a little bit better.

You need to remember a very important fact: Office chairs have wheels.

When he pulled in, I jumped up, ready to smile, defend our riding, offer a hello, or prepare to leave.

Or at least I *tried* to jump up.

In the process of attempting to *leap* to my feet to offer whatever it was I needed to offer, my foot (which had been dutifully planted firmly on the ground just mere seconds before) got hung on one of the 5 legs, *with wheels*, of the chair.

And with what I can only hope is a *shred* of grace and dignity, I went down. I landed on my big ol' belly, but BECAUSE MY FOOT WAS WRAPPED AROUND A CHAIR WITH WHEELS, the chair came rolling right along with me, so that my *only* option (hand to God, it was the only option), was to just drag the chair along for the ride.

When all the commotion stopped, and I had stopped, I looked up to see exactly what kind of first impression I had made on our neighbor.

But since he was bent over double from laughter, I couldn't really tell.....

Life Lesson: Learn to laugh at yourself

So the *rest of the story* is that ... yes, I did get up, and yes, the Preacher was very kind and helpful, and no, I didn't break anything, or get hurt, other than just the jolt from hitting the ground.

But lemme tell ya....Preacher man *could not quit laughing*.

What did *I* do?

Well, when someone is laughing uncontrollably, it's contagious. So I started laughing, too. Pretty soon, we were both laughing so hard, we had tears streaming down our faces and were trying to talk and breathe and not get choked from all that was happening in our heads and bodies.

Learning to laugh *at* myself has been one of the greatest gifts I could give myself because it allows me to be human. I'm not sure what the other option is, but being human means I am not perfect.

I'm barely functional some days, so perfect is definitely out of the question.

Finding humor in the mess-ups, the falls, the goofs, the craziness and chaos of life, means you get to enjoy the mundane and work on your mental health along the way. There's nothing quite like a good belly laugh to make you feel better...science proves it by talking about all that medical and science stuff, but I don't need to know that.

I know that when I laugh at myself, it instantly reduces the stress I'm having, and the stress that anyone else around me is experiencing because *you know* they want to laugh at you, too, but they're holding it in and trying to be nice.

(Ok, your family, your best friends and those random strangers that watched the whole thing go down *are already laughing at you*....just sayin'...)

But lest you think I'm always laughing and finding the funny, know that there have certainly been times I was so mad *at myself*, that I spent precious minutes or even hours belittling and mentally slapping my very being just because something happened outside of what I felt like was the norm.

Ain't *that* crazy?

Yes. Yes it is.

I simply refuse to waste those moments on being mad at myself for something that didn't go right, something I couldn't have seen coming, or even something that I just plain screwed up.

Can I fix it?

Yes.

Should I let it go and just get *on with my life?*

Also yes.

And I should laugh at myself every single chance I get.

You should, too.....you'll be amazed at how good it feels!

Glitter & Grace,
Sasha

Life Guides

Use this guide to remind yourself of how amazing you really are!

Remembering funny stories and details means you get to relive the laughter again. Here, write down 5 times something happened that *could* have made you angry, but you turned it around and laughed instead!

1. _____

   _____

2. _____

   _____

3. _____

   _____

4. _____

   _____

5. _____

   _____

Notes... Doodles... Thoughts on Life

Learn to laugh at yourself

Chapter 11

Saggy Boobs, Bathtubs, and Treadmills

Before we even get into this story, let me say how much I enjoy the age I am now.

I thoroughly appreciate the wisdom, grace, patience, and understanding that goes along with being half a century old plus a little bit more.

But....it's *still* funny when you stop and think about how our body changes as we age. And these words remind us all...

"Old age ain't no place for sissie"s...Bette Davis said those words and I totally agree.

But if you believe all the commercials on TV, you'd think the over 50 crowd is having sex every day (thanks to a little pill) outside in a bathtub after you've come in from playing golf all day and dancing all night at your $900,000 retirement community home.

What we have here, folks, is a little confusion.

And I don't mean confusion because of old age. Nope, I mean the confusion you get from believing everything you see advertised.

So, as a grown up woman that's over 50, I thought it was my responsibility to give you some cold, hard facts about getting older.

Yes, it is great that I've lived to the ripe old age of "Golden"…whatever the THAT means. But there are a few things my body has done since I've turned 50 that I *never* expected.

Now, THAT's confusing.

This list is for all you younger folks out there thinking the time's gonna come when you'll have the luxury of retirement, glowing sunsets, and all the bike rides you can handle. I'm sorry to be the one to break it to you, but there are a few things you need to know:

1. Your body is a traitor. You'll have visions of bounding down the stairs every morning, greeted by your loving spouse, who hands you a cup of coffee with a smile and a kiss. The truth is it'll take you 20 minutes to get up and out of bed, working the kinks out of your knees, hips and back so they'll all move together. Of course, you'll have already pee'd on yourself because you couldn't make it to the bathroom in time because your legs wouldn't move, but hey, what's another quick shower, since you have so much time anyway?

2. Your boobs will become friends with your belly button. Take a picture of your perky boobs NOW, while they're still perky. I don't care if you have tiny boobs or giant boobs, after you hit 50, they just aren't gonna EVER be perky again. Well, not by nature, anyway. And if you were blessed with big girls, they'll become rather oblong and droopy, and if you choose to let 'em

3. hang free, believe me, they'll also be hanging low. Don't wear a crop top.

4. Your eyebrows will thin out, but don't waste time wondering where all the hairs go because you'll be too busy plucking the hairs on your chin and neck. Of course, that's the hairs you can SEE. Most of them are gray now, and you can't see them, so you walk around with a 1" hair growing out of your neck that no one bothers to tell you about. Then one day, you look in the mirror while you're sitting at a stop light and see the beard no one mentioned and scream through 2 green lights while the people behind you blow the horn and flip you off.

5. Speaking of not being able to see, you can't now. Remember when your parents would hold a menu at arm's length so they could read it? Yeah, that's you. Your arms aren't long enough and you can't squint enough to see anything. Just bite the bullet and get the glasses. Of course, the bi-focals will cause you to trip over imaginary lines in the floor and you'll fall over curbs, but "Give it time", they said. Maybe after 2 or 3 years you'll get used to moving your head like you're watching a tennis match every time you try to read a line in a book.

6. You're tired. ALL the time. Suddenly, naps seem like a REALLY good idea. And that's a good thing, because you can fall asleep sitting up MUCH easier now. And if you think you can stay awake long enough to watch anything on TV past 10:00, you're just fooling yourself. You'll be snoring and drooling in that big old recliner way before the 10:00 news comes on. And when you wake up at 3:00 am, fight the urge to buy the Nordic track advertised on the infomercial, because you don't need another clothes rack in the bedroom.

7. All your shoes are slip-ons, because your feet are so much farther away now. It's a medical mystery how that happens, but trust me on this....start buying non-tying shoes NOW. You'll get used to them and won't notice when you can't reach your feet.

Putting on socks is really tough, so go ahead and move to a warmer climate where your feet won't get cold.

8. Which brings me to the last thing: Your internal thermometer is totally whacked out! You're hot. You're cold. You're hot AND cold at the same time. Your feet are cold, but your head is gonna explode from the heat stroke you're having RIGHT NOW. You walk around in socks, shorts and a tank top, with a fan constantly in your hand. In public, you burst into flames and start fanning yourself with whatever you can reach, taking menus from other people and violently waving them in front of yourself, hoping for some relief while others stare wide eyed at your sudden flushed face and wonder if they should dial 911. Ice becomes your friend and you think nothing of dropping a piece down your shirt to cool off, even in winter. Practice saying these words now: "Oh, I spilled my water at lunch. It'll dry soon."

So, old age ain't no place for sissies. It is a place to use your years of experience and accumulated knowledge as you wander through life, offering a hand to the young and unknowing.

Basically, that means try not to scare them as you laugh like a maniac at the thoughts running through your head....

Life Lesson: Love the skin you're in

Show me a woman, and I'll show you someone unhappy with the way they look.

And if I looked in the mirror as recently as 10 years ago, that woman would be me.

I'm over it.

I've always wanted to be skinny (totally an abstract image, determined by fads, social media, all the other media, and the general public and constantly changing).

I was skinny once, but I was 10, and all the kids made fun of me because I was using a piece of string for a belt. In all fairness, mama said it was a ribbon, and it was fashionable, but those mean kids at lunch wouldn't listen.

I have my grandmas fat cells floating through my body and they like it here. They moved in when I was about 12 and decided to stay, stubborn til the end, and fighting against any plan to take them out.

I fought hard and often, waging a war with my soul, bargaining with whoever I thought would help, swearing off all the things that are delicious, and even tossing money at machines and man, only to be deterred again and again.

Losing weight was easy until I hit 30, then my body just laughed and laughed and laughed and said, "Here, have a potato chip and hush".

Then it became a gigantic battle of wills, wit, and workouts, until I decided to see if I could get 'healthier' instead of 'skinnier'. With that mindset switch, my brain accepted the deal, my body relaxed and my soul breathed a giant sigh of relief (and had a brownie).

For me, it's all about balance…a word that gets a full-body workout these days…but it works for me. I can eat the good stuff I absolutely adore, but I try hard not to go crazy and eat the entire bag of potato chips. But if I do, the next day will be much better.

There's too much pressure to look a certain way, and when I hear my 11 year old talk about being 'fat' and needing to go on a diet when she is tall and thin, I know she's heard words, seen pictures, and felt all the disgust piled on anyone who isn't the image of what society thinks we should look like.

I love my wrinkles.

They tell the world (and remind me) that I have laughed and loved, and experienced a life full of wonder.

I love my gray hair.

It shines and sparkles in the sunlight and gives me a look of wisdom I couldn't buy if I tried.

I love my fluffy body.

It shows curves and serves as a comfort for me and those I love.

I'll never be tall and thin, I'll never have a thigh gap, I'll never have that slim neck, full lips, or perfect teeth.

But I love *all* my puzzle pieces and there's no way I'd trade any of them in.

Love all your puzzle pieces….they are what make you who you are. And that's someone that's pretty magical!

Glitter & Grace,
Sasha

Life Guides

Use this guide to remind yourself of how amazing you really are!

It's so easy to name all the things 'wrong' with the image that's looking back at us from the mirror. But today...today I want you to name the things you *love* about that image. Be bold, be brave, be beautiful.

Oh wait...you already are!

1._____

_____

2._____

_____

3._____

_____

4._____

_____

5._____

_____

Notes...Doodles...Thoughts on Life

Love the skin you're in

Chapter 12

Tractors, Nehi Sodas, and Larry

Larry is a veteran.

I know this as a fact, because as I sat on the rough wooden plank that substituted for a bench, my grape Nehi at my feet and the breeze blowing gently under that covered porch of an old general store, Larry sat down for a minute to rest and asked me if I was a nurse.

"No sir, no nurse here."

Larry shrugged and started to remove his shoe and sock, showing me a bruised foot and a large lump on his leg. He told me about tripping on a step and kicking his leg, and how he was sorta worried about it now, because it sure did hurt.

And even though I'm not a nurse, I recognized a painful bruise, but that lump was what would worry me....it looked like what I thought a blood clot would look like and told him so.

He said he was gonna get through the rest of the day at the Tractor show, wiping his brow with the handkerchief tucked in the small square pocket of his overalls. Larry looked out over the crowd, and I imagined him hurrying the day along, anxious to get off his feet and rest.

"I'll go on to Charlotte to the VA on Monday if it don't get no better. They have an x-ray machine there and I can find out what's wrong. Do ya think it's broke?"

"No, sir" I said, "but I think they should check it out, especially that lump on your calf."

Larry laughed, because that lump didn't worry him at all.

These were the kinds of people we met on Saturday at the Tractor show....hard working farmers, and country folk with worn overalls, boots, and leathery skin beneath a denim work shirt or a t-shirt.

We met Scott, who turned a piece of steel into a key ring right before our eyes, hammering the red hot metal with arms that looked like the very steel he was molding. He was at ease in the 90 degree weather, calm and sure with the fire close by. He was generous with his talents and knowledge, showing us each step in the process, as if we could pick up the hammer and recreate what he so easily made.

Three-year-olds competed in the tractor pull, boys and girls alike, some wearing cowboy boots and camo, others in flip flops and shorts.

When I heard the announcement of distances each competitor pulled, I looked in surprise to my husband, who was smiling.

With distances like '7 feet, 3 inches', I knew I had either not watched closely or the measuring they were doing was not something I was familiar with. But they were simply adding a little fun to the competition and glory to a three-year-old's ears....the 'feet' part was merely an add-on.

We watched the winners head to the booth to get their free ice cream cone certificate, 3 little boys in matching jeans, boots and cowboy hats, urging the smallest one on to the "Stairs of Victory".

His smile was wide when the lady in the booth asked for his drivers license because she was sure he was a professional driver.

Men with thick gloves handled logs larger than they were, stacking and turning to get the trunk in line with the saw blade, which was pulled with a steam engine, just like the old days. They thought nothing of the heat, the sawdust flying and the blade of a giant saw inches away.

A young boy, probably 10-years-old, stood by ready to clean up dropped bark and splinters of wood almost as big as he was.

There was music...three men under the shade from a porch of an old house, the flag flying proudly in front. A banjo and 2 guitar players, with bales of hay for seats and the occasional camp chair close by, tuned up and prepared to entertain the folks that stopped by after the tractor pulling races were over.

Ham and steak biscuits were on the menu, along with coconut pie, the menu a chalk board propped against the edge of a covered shack with canned sodas sitting close by, ready to quench the thirst of the hot, sweaty crowd.

Inside the general store, a long, lean cooler, full of bottled Nehi drinks, stood sturdy, as it has stood for years. The two concession trucks offered what every kid wants...sno cones, cotton candy, popcorn and funnel cakes. Sticky mouths and stickier hands were attached to little boys and girls and sometimes big boys and girls, too.

There was a field full of antique and new tractors, each with a tag attached, the owner's name prominently displayed, with facts and figures listed. They weren't for sale, but merely show, and you could tell a lot of them were ridden in off the field the day before.

My feet were dirty from the grass and field, but my soul was full.

The people were friendly, kind, generous and happy. As quick to share a story as their seat, the old timer in me listened with a hunger for a time that will be whisked away one day.

My hopes are those 3-year-old tractor pulling champs will still be hanging out in the field when they're Larry's age and have stories to tell their grandchildren about the time when.....

Life Lesson: Always be as kind as possible

In my younger years, I was hell bent and whiskey bound to always be right, always be the one in charge, always have the last word and be louder, taller, and stronger than anyone else.

Bless My Heart....

To say I've mellowed over the years would be a giant understatement. Thanks to medications when I needed them, a *lot* of inward reflection, the discovery of life coaching and just the empathy that comes with age, I have changed my wily ways.

When I think back to some of the past transgressions in my life, I don't look back with regret or shame because that's who I was then. I can spend the rest of my days in hiding, regretting something I said or did, OR I can spend the rest of my days living my life as I want to live it now: Kinder, gentler, funnier, happier.

I think the universe will reap the rewards of me being those things rather than living with the regrets of my past. And while I can't change anything that happened in my prior life, I can reach out when possible to those I cast a shadow on, and I can also touch the lives of people I meet every day.

I've discovered I can always be kinder. Even in the worst of situations, when a strong, firm stand is needed and we have to be a force to be reckoned with, my word choices and my actions have to be guided by my life and how I live it.

And with age, comes wisdom.

No longer do I need to always be right, or have the last word, or make sure everyone knows what I'm thinking.

Part of that is being secure and confident in who you are, and not necessarily needing the approval of others. I honestly don't care what others think of me.

To get to *that* phase of life is one of the most freeing places I've ever been and it's been a long, winding journey to get here. And while I don't care what others think of me, my style, my opinions or any of the thousands of other things people seem to care about these days, I do want to offer kindness where I can, hope where it's possible, and a smile to anyone I see.

Those things make *me* feel good about being in the universe, and make me want to leave a legacy that reminds others to do the same.

And, almost always....kindness doesn't cost a thing.

Glitter & Grace,
Sasha

122

Life Guides

Use this guide to remind yourself of how amazing you really are!

I believe kindness really does matter. I also believe we are better for receiving it and better for giving it whenever possible. Let this be a 'bucket list of kindness'....list 5 ways you can show kindness to someone this week.

1. _____
   _____

2. _____
   _____

3. _____
   _____

4. _____
   _____

5. _____
   _____

Notes... Doodles... Thoughts on Life

Always be as kind as possible

Chapter 13

Fried Chicken, Goals, and Crossing Yards

Walking back from Daddy's after a late lunch, I was attacked by a stick.

Now I didn't KNOW it was a stick when it happened, so I was sure it was some wild animal, vicious and relentless in its stealth as my demise was planned and plotted.

I was walking along, carrying the extra fried chicken wrapped in tin foil (Oh! You thought I *made* the fried chicken? Bwahahahaha), my tea glass firmly held in the crook of my arm, and Tater's Capri Sun dangling from 2 fingers.

I looked back to make sure Tater was behind me and as I took that next step, mere feet from the safety of my own front porch, I stepped in the trap of the little known, rarely seen, but often rumored to-be-deadly, "Stickintheground".

The moment I stepped in its nest, it reared its ugly arm and slapped my ankle to let me know I had angered the beast.

Naturally, I screamed and dropped the Capri Sun (but not the Fried Chicken because that would have been a sin), threw my arm up, jumped about 3 feet (ok, I skipped a little but it *should* have been about 3 feet) and started swatting at my legs, while looking for the wild beast that attacked me.

Mac was already at the porch and turned around to see why I had screamed. (However, he didn't come rushing ....hmmmm...).

I told him about the wild animal, sure he would come running to save me from a certain horrible death.

He looked at the ground, looked at me, looked at the ground.....looked back at me.

"Honey, it's just a stick. You stepped on a stick" as bubbles of laughter began to cascade from him, even as he was trying NOT to laugh. Tater had caught up to me by then and even she was laughing.

So I did what any normal, self-respecting, slightly stressed, maybe strange, and perhaps tired, woman would do: I went over to that stick, stomped on it about 20 times, then picked it up and broke it into a bazillion tiny pieces and ever-so-calmly walked over to the fire pit where I let it fall from my hands like a baptism of fear mixed with victory.

My slightly shocked family watched me pick up the foil wrapped fried chicken (of course I laid it down...taking no chance of ruining that chicken), walk into the house and carry on because killing a wild animal in the middle of a Sunday afternoon is just how I roll.

Life Lesson: Know where you're going

I've said it's important to bring your past self along for the ride because she's the one that's gonna show you the path, guide you when you falter and hold your hand when you cross the rapids of life.

So I *do* believe it's a good plan to look behind you to see where you've been, remind yourself of what you've already accomplished and see the landscape now that it has had the pleasure of you crossing over it in times of mightiness and times of sorrow.

But….it's also very important to know where you're going.

Because, after all, if you don't know where you're going, how will you know when you get there?

As someone who plans almost every second of life (a habit I'm working to lessen, even if it's only slightly), the location of where I'm going is *extremely* important to me. I want to make sure I know when I get there, I have planned for the arrival time and I also know what I'm going to *do* when I get there and a plan to make it happen.

Yeah, that's kinda nuts.

So, you do you, babe!

Along the way, take the time to make a plan, and have a goal. It doesn't have to be this gigantic bucket list of goals, or something that you're going to focus the next 10 years on, but at least have an *idea* of where you want to be in 1 year, 5 years, even 10 years and when you have THAT part down, then you can think about the journey you'll take to get there, how that looks on your travel plans and what you need to make it so.

One thing you'll need to remember as you make this loose prediction for your future: It will change.

A lot.

You'll be surprised how your goals, dreams, and hopes will move to higher levels and how some will drop off completely because they just aren't who you are right now.

And that's a really good thing....because it means *you* are growing, and changing, and learning along the way.

So think big! Think outside the box, around the box, under the box and on top of the box....just make sure you jot those big ideas down somewhere so you'll be able to go back and look at them in 6 weeks, 6 months, or 6 years so you can see how far you've grown!

Glitter & Grace,
Sasha

Life Guides

Use this guide to remind yourself of how amazing you really are!

For me, writing down my goals is a BIG deal. I need to *see* them laid out on paper, to remind me that THIS is what I'm going for. So, right here, right now, write down 5 goals you have. It doesn't matter if you've never thought of them before or whether they are too big or too small. The first step is writing them down.

1._____

_____

2._____

_____

3._____

_____

4._____

_____

5._____

_____

Notes...Doodles...Thoughts on Life

Know where you're going

Chapter 14

Legos, Book Fairs, And Finding Joy

I had lunch with a special little 6-year-old boy today.

I sat on the small round stool, (too close to the ground for my old knees), and straddled the bar holding up my end of the table.

The voices carried across the high ceiling of the lunchroom, excitement in the air as the book fair happened in the room next door and lunches were forgotten as friends bartered for chips brought from home, and raced to see who could drink milk the fastest.

I saw the smallest lego, proudly held in tiny, dirty hands covered in cheese and tomato sauce, waved in front of my face with the urgency to "Look at the back! Look at the back". When I turned it over, I saw it was the tiniest batman logo ever and pride swelled in the young man as he held the prized piece.

Signs of 'no running' and 'use your quiet voice' were ignored as little legs returned for forks and napkins, and high fives were accompanied by loud choruses of "YES" and "HEY JORDAN, sit by me!".

The Chicken pot pie (strongly suggested by the teacher helping to keep the line moving - thankyouverymuch) was absolutely delicious and I found myself wondering if this was standard fare for this lunchroom or this special visitors day (conveniently tied to a book sale) brought out all the goodness. Even the chicken wrap my lunch buddy had looked great and the sweet potato wedges were equally good....although I was informed that the potato wedges were much better.

This last piece of information was whispered in my ear, tiny hands grasping the edges of my hair to make sure I was close enough to hear, not wanting anyone else to know of preferences and perhaps dislike to today's meal.

After lunch, the book fair was our target, and excitement ramped up to epic levels when the possibilities appeared endless. I had a list, sent over by mom, of what was allowed, but that made no difference.

After I showed the list, calmly (but loudly in the not so quiet library turned retail store), explained that he had to pick something that was on the list, we bargained a little, and I agreed to agree to a deal....one book ON the list and one book OFF the list.

He proudly carried his plastic bag with his 2 books and the receipt held tightly in still dirty hands, showing me the way to his room and his friends.

We wound through the halls, his shorter legs still faster than my older, longer ones. I noticed the "o" signs in the hall, indicating there was no talking allowed, but I didn't see that rule followed very closely, as parents roamed around, led by small people filled with the excitement of new things and new people in familiar places.

Just as we got to his room, the teacher was lining up the other students for a bathroom break, and as he took his place, he paused to show his friends his prized new purchases.

As I turned to leave, he ran up one more time, yelled "Sasha" and gave me a big hug.

And then his world returned to 1st grade, book fares and reading, writing, and 'rithmatic.

My world turned to finding my out of the elementary school hall maze, turning in my visitors sticker and smiling as I walked to my car.....

Life Lesson: Little things matter

"Stop and smell the roses"
"Just enjoy life"
"You'll miss all the good times"

All these quotes remind us to slow down and take a hot minute to just *be*.

I'm not always good at just *be-ing*, because my plate is always full, my time limited and my to-do list way too long.

But every single time I get to experience the joy of 'the little things', I remember the power in those moments as a reminder that life is hectic, life is chaotic, and life is crazy....and if we can occasionally get off the merry-go-round and look at the world from the bleachers, it's a very good thing.

Have mercy, HOW do we get *there*, though? We continue to pile on more things to the list, accept more responsibilities and have totally forgotten how to say "No" because we think it's a slap to our ability to adult when we are unable to do #allthethings.

And that, my friend, is crazy town.

For me, it begins with answering a few questions....questions I can come back to again and again, realizing they are the base for my 'little things moments'. and the answers to these simple questions help guide me when I forget how to stop and get off the train.

- What brings you joy? This is a question you should ask yourself often and when you discover the *real* answer, repeat it over and over. And then you can change it to: What brings me (insert what brings you joy)?
- Will I be able to keep my commitments if I escape for an hour/half a day/day/weekend/however long you can get away?
- Does my mental, physical, emotional, or spiritual being *need* this break from every day life?
- What changes if I stop for a short while?

If you want to only ask yourself one question, let it be: Does this bring me joy?

Really, you could ask that question before you decide to tackle any new adventure, or set up your goals and dreams.

I know not everything will bring you joy, and some things will actually take you so far away from joy that you'll wonder when you'll ever see it again. But if your goal is always to seek joy (or wonder, love, utopia...whatever your word is), then you'll be driven back to it every single time simply by asking that question.

And I'm gonna bet all my money on you and living your best life as the ultimate 'little thing'.

Glitter & Grace,
Sasha

Life Guides

Use this guide to remind yourself of how amazing you really are!

Whatever it is that you seek...joy, wonder, adventure, shenanigans, utopia...you have to first know what that means *to you*.

List 5 things that bring you joy (or whatever you're seeking)...start here and then make a plan to get them!

1._____

_____

2._____

_____

3._____

_____

4._____

_____

5._____

_____

Notes...Doodles...Thoughts on Life

Little things matter

Chapter 15

Race Cars, Chances, and Fuel for your Fears

When I was in-between Husbands, a single mom and working 3 jobs to make ends meet, I found myself managing a concession stand at a local race track.

The work was 1 day a week, on Friday nights from 4:00 pm until around 2:00 am….it was running wide open the entire time and I made sure there were people to toss food out the tiny windows, enough fries to feed hundreds and always full tanks of cherry syrup to mix with the Mtn. Dew for a sweeter-than-sugar drink all the locals craved.

The race track owner was also a race car driver and one early morning, under the brightly lit track, with the smell of fuel, mangled steel, and hot grease still pungent in the air, he was running laps in a small race car, the roar of the engine the only sound in the hot summer night.

He pulled to the infield, where I was standing impatiently waiting to be paid and asked if I wanted to "take it for a spin".

Absoflippinlutely.

I climbed in the car, strapped in with a 5 buckle harness and put on a helmet that God only knew whose head it had graced a few hours prior.

And with a slap on the side of the car, I was off, racing around that track at 90 mph, the wind whipping my hair through the open windows, as I shifted gears and felt the breath leave my soul around every curve.

I coasted to a stop as he waved me in after 3 laps, still flying high from the adrenaline of speed, being in the right place at the right time and fighting the track for speed and control. As I climbed out of the car, he gave me a high five, asked me if I had fun, then laughed when I squealed a little and jumped up and down (I was *much* younger then, and jumping up and down was totally doable…).

And right then and there, out loud for God and anyone else to hear, I thanked my mama for teaching me to drive a stick shift when I was 10-years-old.

Life Lesson: Do it Afraid

You might have heard that I'm a planner….like, plan everything to the nth degree (what degree is that, exactly?) and leave nothing to chance.

So saying "Do It Afraid" isn't something I say lightly, easily, or even very loudly. But I like to push it out there, letting it scoot near the edge of maybe and see what happens.

But Fear is a real emotion, and every single one of us has experienced it.

Fear actually keeps us safe….it's a response to potential danger and helps guide us to safety. So it's not a bad thing when you feel fear, but it can be a very limiting thing if you allow it to keep you from doing something you love, something you want to do, or going where you belong.

It would be foolish to toss all fear aside and go through life with total abandon…you'd soon be watching chaos reign all over your place, random people trying to catch you as you fall, and looks of worry from everyone you know.

But, when we are *so* afraid to take a step into the unknown that we are paralyzed by it and remain stuck where we've always been, then that's the opposite end of the spectrum and that's not a place I want to be.

Can you plan for every option, yet still be afraid to take that step?

Most definitely.

Will you allow that to stop you from living your best life?

I hope not.

Every single thing we do has a risk. Think about it…driving to work, walking in your office, cooking, bathing, being alive during a dangerous storm….nothing is totally safe.

Yet, every day we do those things because we are *living*.

We minimize the risk by being informed, being careful, gaining all the knowledge we can about whatever it is we're doing, and we go out and live life.

We still get hurt. Tragedy still strikes, and crazy things happen.

We could never leave the proposed safety of our own home, thinking that would keep us safe, but I don't have to tout the statistics about home invasions, and weird freak accidents to remind you it's not always safest there either.

By being informed, by being aware, by being cautious (not *overly*), we can minimize the risks of life.

But if we never step out and try something new out of fear, then think what we might be missing out on.....

It might be 90 mph in a race car on a black top at 2:00 am.

And that's something I am thrilled I didn't miss!

Glitter & Grace,
Sasha

Life Guides

Use this guide to remind yourself of how amazing you really are!

What has fear kept you from doing? List 5 things that you've always wanted to do, but haven't because you were afraid.

Then...start a plan to make them happen!

1. _____

   _____

2. _____

   _____

3. _____

   _____

4. _____

   _____

5. _____

   _____

Notes... Doodles... Thoughts on Life

Do it afraid

One More Thing

These stories, life lessons, guides, and color sheets I've offered here were brought to these pages with much love, joy, humor, and passion. My goal was to impart some of the life lessons I've learned the hard way...not so you wouldn't have to endure the lesson yourself, but so that you might gain insight in your own journey as you travelled this life of yours.

The stories are part of *my* journey and keep me laughing....and laughing is where my joy comes from, how I survive this crazy, chaotic world and what I enjoy seeing others do most when I'm speaking.

Before I go, I have one more thing I'd like to share with you that isn't a life lesson, doesn't have a guide for you to complete and I didn't even include a color sheet (the nerve!).

What I have to offer you, at the end of the day, is my wish for you. It doesn't matter if we've never met, if we'd never even heard of each other before you picked up this book or hung out with me on social media or if we'll never cross paths at any part of our shared journey.

I still wish this for you...

Glitter & Grace,
Sasha

I want you to prosper. Not just survive, but thrive and prosper and glow again, or for the first time. I want you to know what it's like to succeed on your own and be your own woman. I want you to have the drive, the determination, the goals, and the tenacity to get up every single day and do everything you have to do to get to the prospering place, wherever that may be.

I want you to be a better person than you were the day before and know that, because of your journey, and in spite of all you've been through, you will remember how far you've come. You're a good person, a great person, but we ALL can be a better person. We just have to stop, look around and see what we want for ourselves to be better and go after that.

I want you to distance yourself from those in your life that drain you emotionally, physically, and financially, so you can rise above pettiness, drama and the energy sucking that goes along with those people. That's not to mean they're not in your life, but it means they no longer hold any control over your feelings or actions.

I want you to adjust your attitude about everything that has ever happened to you to one of 'experience' instead of one of 'why me?'. *Everything* you've been through up to this very moment in your life has shaped you to where you are RIGHT now. It's that way for all of us. We screw up, we learn, we do differently. You'll never stop screwing up, none of us will. But if we use that screw up as a learning experience, then we've bettered ourselves and won't be as likely to make that same screw up again. Or, at the very least, we'll be able to look at it differently.

I want you to look at each day as an opportunity. Attack it. Live it. Dream it. Look for something good in every single day, because it's there. Sometimes it's hard to find, but it *is* there. And sometimes, it's so damn tiny, that you have to squint to see it, but you'll find it. And then, if that's the only good thing about the day, you'll have something to smile about.

I want you to plan your destiny. Of course, destiny, karma and the forces of the universe will laugh, but if you have a plan, a realistic one and a dream driven one, then at least you can get back on track or know the path to take when all those other forces laugh. Or...you'll be able to look at your plan and say, "Hey...maybe I should take THIS path instead."

I want you to have something that makes you happy. Something just for you. A secret 'thing' that can make you smile when you pause and see it, or feel it or think about it. This is your sanctuary in this crazy, messed up world we live in. Pick a place and visualize it then keep it tucked in your memory for those moments when you just can't take any more. See it, think it, and know you'll get through this, too.

And Last, but certainly not least....I want you find love. But I want it to be the self love you carry with you every single day, the love that allows you to be the self confident woman you are, and the kind of love that shines out of you so brightly, others will smile just seeing you walk in a room.

May you dream big, laugh loudly, and love yourself every single day!

AUTHOR INFO

As a Speaker, Author, Master Certified Life Coach, Certified Business Coach and Motivational Mindset Mentor for individuals and business owners, Sasha Gray specializes in finding the positive in a negative world and helping others rediscover their self confidence, kick the self doubt, and use humor along their journey to make even the roughest roads smooth.

But that doesn't really tell you who she is, does it?

Maybe these bullet points will help:
- She's a Sassy Southern Belle
- She's never met a stage she didn't love
- Her favorite color is Glitter
- She loves to tell a story
- Wait! Purple is her favorite color
- She speaks sarcasm and Southern fluently
- Her favorite exercise is running her mouth
- She uses too many emojis in every text message
- Iced Caramel Macchiato and Sweet Tea are her best friends

She is fueled by a desire to live her best life and bring humor, glitter and a whole lot of real life to everything she does. Since Life decided to toss a ridiculous amount of chaos, crazy, and commotion into her world, she decided to toss it back and ask for chocolate and margaritas instead.

Life laughed, said, "deal with it" and left her with Karma and all the things that go along with juggling the care of an aging parent, a pre-teen daughter, a traveling salesman, and one crazy dog.

Her goal is to share the tools needed to navigate this crazy thing called life while being successful in every part of it. And if you laugh along your journey, then that means you're winning.

To connect:
www.scatteredsasha.com
fb/Scattered Sasha
YouTube/Scattered Sasha
IG/Scattered Sasha
sasha@scatteredsasha.com

Y'all....I just couldn't....

I've been writing this book my entire life.

I just didn't know it.

It wouldn't have been possible without the help of some very special people in my life and I'm going to do my best to thank them here.

My family...those people that live in the same house, at least part of the time. If they hadn't left me alone to actually let me write, it would have never happened. (Oh yeah...and they never thought I was too crazy for trying to do this. Well, at least they never *said* they thought that...) I'll try to write the next book when you're not home...

Friends in the online space that held me up, said the good words I needed to hear, never doubted I could do anything I put my mind to and were always willing to read whatever I put out there, and tell me the truth about it. I will undoubtedly leave someone out, but here's my best shot at getting it right: Alexa, Rachel, Kate, Rachael, Melissa, Lizzy, Angie, Heather, Adri, Jessica, Tara, Renee, Debbie, and Carrie.

There are many more that chatted, answered, talked through, and just listened and I am forever grateful for you all, the online space that allows us this connection and your willingness to hear a girl out.

I owe all y'all a margarita.

To my biz bestie Leslie that never fails to build me up and remind me of my own words when needed. Lunch is on me next time.

To the friends that read every word I wrote, proofed it for me, and then re-read it again just because they said they liked it ... Kate and Robin, I promise to get you red pens for the next time. When we finally get to have lunch together, I'll buy the wine.

To the FBG's....my soul mates, my life lines, my never-fail-to-help-me friends that have been there through it all. Time doesn't allow us the space we need to gather as often as we should. Let's change that this year. Where are we going, and who's making the arrangements?

And finally, to the ones that hang out with me on my Facebook page, watched hours and hours of the Scattered Sasha Show and the Morning Y'all Show, laughed with me and at me and reminded me that there really are good people out there. Thank you from the bottom of my heart. I promise to continue to give you laughter and love, glitter and grace as long as you'll let me.

Glitter & Grace,
Sasha